Cricut for Beginners

The best tips and craft ideas to get started with your cutting machine!

Contents

Introduction

Chapter 1: The Cricut Machines and Their Popularity

Chapter 2: Explaining the Different Models of Cricut Machines

Chapter 3: Explaining How to Use a Cricut Machine

Chapter 4: Explaining What Cricut Design Space Is and How to Use It to Create Your Own Custom Projects

Conclusion

Introduction

You made the right choice in purchasing "Cricut for Beginners!" The reason why is because the book is full of details about the Cricut® machine. Not only will it provide a basic understanding of the machine and the materials it can cut and create, but it also provides you with a selection to choose from for all your crafting and hobby needs.
The book starts off by providing you with a great introduction to what Cricut is and why it has become so popular recently. Then it goes into the various Cricut models and gives a detailed description of each.
We then go into explaining how to use the Cricut machine. We will explore the exclusive app that is utilized by the Cricut machines known as "Cricut Design Space™" and how you can easily use it to create awesome projects that are custom-made.
In chapter 5, we explain the basics of Cricut techniques and materials you can cut for your first cut, and we will explain what supplies you need to get started. Finally, in chapter 6, we explain what kind of projects you can make with a Cricut machine.
This all may seem like a lot to take in, but you can be reassured that this book will guide you throughout the process of doing craft projects that you will be proud of.

Chapter 1: The Cricut Machines and Their Popularity

If you love crafting, then chances are you have heard about the Cricut machines and all the wonderful things that you can create with them. If you have heard of the Cricut machine, then you are more than likely thinking of buying one soon. Or, perhaps you obtained one and are now in need of some guide to find out everything about it.

If this is the case for you, then there will be no problem with you getting the most out of this chapter. I will help do a quick rundown about the Cricut with the goal that you can see all the wonderful ways to deal with it and utilize this workstation in your crafting needs.

Since Cricut started, there are presently a bunch of Cricut machines to choose from. So, which one do you need?

All things considered, let me walk you through differentiation data to give you a chance to find the ideal machine for your needs.

Machine Comparison Guide

Maker: Cricut Maker® right away and unequivocally cuts more than 300 hundred materials, from the most unobtrusive paper and material to the troublesome stuff like matboard, calfskin, and basswood. Presently, the inventiveness you can reach with it is exponential.
Explore Air: The performance of Cricut Explore® Air meets esteem. The Cricut Explore Air offers you the expert quality outcomes you need with the additional solace of Bluetooth network for Wi-Fi cuts and a twofold instrument holder for a messiness-free condition.
Explore Air 2: Cricut Explore® Air 2 is "two" times faster than all the other models. It is able to cut a lot more, as well as many other types of material, including iron-on, vinyl, and cardstock.
Explore One: Cricut Explore® One is an astute cutting figuring gadget for DIY activities and specialties that is anything but difficult to break down and simple to utilize. It can cut and write on over 100 types of materials. For example, cardstock, vinyl, and iron-on.

Cricut Maker

The Cricut Maker is the most up-to-date, propelled Cricut workstation, and it has a ton of incredible highlights. They are fundamentally the same as the Explore line; however, they appear to lift a couple of more noteworthy advantages.

- **Rotary Blade:** They offer a Cricut Rotary Blade that will cut unbounded materials. With that capacity, you needn't bother with a stabilizer, as the Explore machines require.
- **Scoring Wheel:** This is a pleasant improvement from the Scoring Stylus. It saves time and leaves a smooth line.
- **Knife Blade:** You can utilize this to cut thicker calfskin and even materials like balsa wood. This is a top-notch machine.
- **Basic Perforation Blade:** It leaves better tear-offs and easy strip-away utilizing paper, cardstock, acetic acid derivation, notice board—and that's only the tip of the iceberg.

- **Wavy Blade:** It can quickly make a charming wavy zone on a range of well-known materials.
- **Fine Debossing Tip:** You can use this to customize activities with fresh, specific debossed structures—no crucial envelopes.
- **Engraving Tip:** This can engrave uncommon and everlasting structures on a range of materials.

Moreover, Cricut presented in July 2019 that there will be a huge amount of new items pushed out to be available. When I get my hands on them, you can unwind guaranteed that we will teach you how to create your projects using those new items in the Cricut line!

Explore Air and Explore Air 2

Both of these machines are a more prominent minimal effort alternative. Explore machines enable you to work with a range of materials for your creations: Vinyl, cardstock, foil, sparkle paper, reinforced fabric, and the sky is the limit from there. The biggest difference between the Explore Air and the Explore Air 2 is the size contrast. The Explore Air 2 is a big machine.

Explore One

The Explore One is a workstation that I recommend to tenderfoots at crafting.
There are confined aspects anyway adequate that you can make and format exceptional crafts. This is the most reduced rate factor, too, so in the event that you are on a value go, this ought to be a perfect starter machine. At that point, as you study and develop, you can generally improve later to one of the other machines.
Any of the machines are great, so it depends on what format to utilize it for, the materials you have, and what sort of crafts you want to make.

Which Cricut Is Best?

Cricut Maker: This is the one if you need every one of the fancy items and a fast and quiet machine.
Explore Air 2: This is an affordable yet impressive machine that can meet the crafter's needs!

Cricut has an absolute slew of items and materials. I adore Cricut Infusible Inks and Vinyl Projects; these are likely my top picks. What's more, they make planning easy with Cricut Design Space™.

Possibly, you got a Cricut workstation for Christmas or a birthday; however, it's as yet sitting in its container. Or, on the other hand, maybe you're an eager crafter looking for a straightforward gadget to make crafting simpler. Or, maybe you've considered huge amounts of cool pictures on Pinterest and pondered, "How the hell do they decrease those muddled plans? I want to do that!" Or maybe you've known about Cricut, yet you're asking, "What is a Cricut machine, and what would you be able to do with it?" Well, you're in the correct spot because I will acquaint you with the Cricut Explore Air machine and tell you pretty much all the cool things it can do!

There are no additional cartridges; the entire parcel is done carefully so you can utilize any textual style or structure that is on your PC. What's more, the greater part of the Cricut machines is that they work over Wi-Fi or Bluetooth, so you can outline from your iPhone or iPad just as from your PC! The Cricut machines are helpful to utilize, totally adaptable, and exclusively provided with the guide that you need for all your inventiveness!

What Is a Cricut Machine?

The Cricut Explore Air is a must-have on cutting workstations (otherwise known as specialist plotters or cutting machines). You can consider it like a printer; you take a photo or design on your PC and afterward send it to the machine. The Cricut Explore Air can cut paper (including sticker paper), vinyl, fabrics, craft foam, and faux leather — and that's only the tip of the iceberg!

Truth be told, if you like to utilize a Cricut like a printer, it can do that as well! There is a highlight opening in the machine, and you can stack a marker in there, and after that, have the Cricut "draw" your plan for you. It's ideal for getting a top-notch result written by hand if your penmanship isn't too extraordinary. The Cricut Explore® series favors you to get admission to a really large advanced library of "cartridges" rather than utilizing physical cartridges, as I did in school. This implies that you can utilize Cricut Design Space™ (the online format programming) to take any content or shape from the library and send it to your Cricut. You can even transfer your own plans if you need to!

The Cricut Explore Air can slice materials up to 12 inches and has a little cutting blade introduced inward the machine. When you're prepared to cut something, you load the material onto a clingy mat called "cutting mat" and then place the mat into the machine. The mat holds the material while the Cricut cuts it. When it has finished cutting, you remove the mat from the machine, take the material off the mat, and you're ready to go!

With a Cricut machine, the possibilities are infinite! All you need is a Cricut machine, Design Space™, something to cut, and your own innovativeness!

What Can I Do with a Cricut Machine?

There are tons of things you can do with a Cricut machine! It is absolutely impossible for me to rundown every one of the potential outcomes, but anyway, here are a couple of renowned sorts of activities to give you an idea of what the machine can do.

It can…

- cut out energizing shapes and letters for scrapbooking.
- make custom, carefully assembled playing cards for any uncommon event.
- design a onesie or a shirt.
- make a cowhide-based wrist trinket.
- make buntings and distinctive birthday festivity embellishments.
- create your own stencils for depictions.
- make a vinyl clingy name for your car window.
- label stuff in your washroom, or in a den.
- make monogram cushions.
- create your own Christmas enhances.
- address an envelope.
- decorate a mug, cup, or tumbler.
- etch glass at home.
- create your very own divider decals.
- make a painted wooden sign.
- make your own special window sticks.
- cut appliqués or blanket squares.
- create decals for a stand blender.
- do stacks of different undertakings that are too much to list!

Why it Has Become So Popular Today

The Cricut Maker is the most recent machine from the Cricut Cutting Machine family! This new workstation is incredible nowadays. I'm sharing my top 11 reasons you'll adore the Cricut Maker, and it's more prominent than just the marvelous Cricut projects you might have the option to make! From paper and vinyl to wood and fabric, there are no limits for the things you can make!

You remember, we value the Cricut Explore Air 2 for all its top-notch cutting and creating capacities. Well, you will now meet the big sister, and she's solid, inventive, and prepared to make all the Cricut activities into the late evening! (Or, on the other hand, till you come up short on coffee and head to sleep). The Cricut maker is the Cricut Explore with an all-out new arrangement of abilities. I believe you're going to love her!

These reasons will have you cherishing Cricut. The Cricut Maker is fast, fantastic, and furnished to work with fabrics! I was competent to see it live and face to face on an ongoing occasion facilitated by the Cricut group in Salt Lake City. The issues you have come to adore about the Cricut Explore family are all together in any case there. Presently there's even an extra to cherish. For every person that needs the intricate details and the how's and whys, I'm clarifying those things about each machine. How about we go?

The Best 11 Reasons Why You'll Fall in Love with Cricut

- **Reasonable Yet Better:** They are the same machines at the center with more highlights and power to challenge conceivable outcomes.
- **It Cuts Fabric:** It has a blade specially designed to cut fabric tests (Bonded Fabric Blade), and a has a mat specially designed to support fabric.
- **Sewing Examples from Effortlessness:** 100's of sewing designs are reachable in Configuration Space (with crease remittances).
- **Rotatory Blade:** It is used to cut materials in a wide range of sensitive materials.
- **Fine-Point Blade:** It is used to cut heavy-duty materials like balsa and birchwood.
- **Versatile Machine Framework:** It is used to take into consideration additional cutting controls and additional items later on.
- **More Stockpiling:** The special Explore stockpiling is new and extended to give more noteworthy choices.
- **Print on Colored Paper:** You can print on colored paper with Print then Cut plans.
- **Gadget Holder and Charger:** This is a region on the apex of the PC to hold your units and a charging port so you can cost while you make.

- **iOs and Android Applications:** iOs and Android can be used in a hurry!
- **Wonderful Plan Subtleties:** The Cricut machines have the same dazzling portrayal and printing capabilities, with the one of a kind Explore being a little more prominent.

Top 11 Reasons—The Detailed List

If the short descriptions above aren't enough, well, here are them again, but this time more detailed.

The Cricut machines are dazzling, and they have adequate flexibility and capacity to help make the undertakings you like to make. From paper artworks to little carpentry extends, these machines can make such a large number of particular plans and activities with you!

Reasonable Yet Better: The Cricut Maker is the same magnificent machine as the Explore Air 2; however, shockingly better! Alright, this really is anything but another "reason" to cherish another machine. Aside from this, it is the additional fundamental reason why I cherish this new machine. I, as of now, love my Cricut Explore Air 2. I cherish the use of Configuration Space, and I'm in all actuality satisfied with all the imaginative energizing I can have with this machine. The Cricut Maker is, however, far and away superior. There are more prominent highlights and additional capabilities. It can do things that I, as of now, love and new things that I want to try. Continue examining this machine, and you'll understand.

The Cricut Maker Cuts Fabric: The new Cricut Maker has been reengineered to work with fabric. It comes outfitted and arranged to work with another rotary cutting blade and a one of a kind cutting mat. You read that right… fabric! I perceive that a few people have been cutting fabric with their Cricut machines. I haven't had a lot of luck with it. I've typically wanted to cut fabrics that I use in my sewing projects, appliques, designs, and so on. Presently, the Cricut Maker has been sketched to do just that! I tried its cutting capabilities, and they are delightful. The same applies if you cut by hand! Not a sewer? Forget about it! Crafters can join the understanding that there is no fabric we cannot work on with the use of our Cricut. I haven't found one type of fabric that I cannot cut with my Cricut.

Sewing Examples from Effortlessness: You can find these sewing examples in Configuration Space.

Rotatory Blade: This sharp blade cuts fabric easily. It will likewise be you're a fine companion for cutting refined materials. I hear it can cut crepe paper splendidly! So, think. You're never again simply compelled to extravagant cardstock and specialty papers. We should test it with every one of the substances from tissue paper to balsawood; the Cricut can adapt to it!

Fine-Point Blade: It can cut thicker substances this the new blade. It can cut balsa wood, birchwood, thicker cardboard, and even chipboard. Your imagination can go even likewise with more noteworthy materials and cutting alternatives!

Versatile Device Framework: So you, as of now, analyze that the new Cricut Maker includes a Rotary Blade and a Fine-Point Blade. This new Cricut machine has been intended to empower more prominent hardware as the group envisions additional gear to include in the machine. So, as they assume up additional approaches to enable you to make your creations, the machine is set up for new hardware to be included; you'll simply need to sit back and watch what's straightaway!

More Stockpiling: The pen holder on the Maker has been overhauled to protect your instruments and embellishments. There is a deep cup and a shallow cup to hold a range of things effectively. Also, the in-entryway complement holder has furthermore been overhauled to include a couple of additional compartments, so all your Cricut adornments have a home!

It Prints on Shaded Paper: What!? Truly, it is valid. The Print Then Cut capacity is matched with the Cricut Maker to take into account imprinting on shaded and designed paper. You never again are limited to printing your Cricut projects on white paper. So, proceed, get imaginative, print layers of workmanship, and cut your materials!

Gadget Holder and Charger: We utilize these versatile units with Cricut machines, and now the Maker has an area to put those gadgets while you chip away at our undertakings. Set your phone, for example, in this holder at the apex of the machine. What's more, there is a USB port on the Maker so you can connect your gadgets and charge them while you are crafting; helpful, I state!

iOs and Android Applications: You can set up your cut plans from any place with the cell applications, which are supported for both iOs and Android. Effectively, make the formats you want to make on your iPhone and transfer them later to your PC. You can send plans to the machine through these cell applications, or you can update your Structure Space account and upload the files later.

Delightful Plan Subtleties: Really, the design is considerably prettier, and the measurement is marginally greater with the Cricut Maker. The Cricut Maker will, by and by, fit in your carrier case and should, in any case, fit on your favorite art rack. They've also ensured some additional extravagant bling and finishing.

All the New Things About the Cricut Maker

Let's face it, no longer does everybody cherish change, as we as of now love or are satisfied with what we have. So here's the thing: There's a couple of things that are changing with the new Cricut Maker that you may wind up asking yourself, "For what reason did they do that?"

I've obtained answers for you! What's more, I assume these are considerably more noteworthy motivations to cherish this new machine:

- **Not Any More Open Catch:** Yes! The open catch is no more. To open the entryways on the machine, you plainly lift up the top entryway, and the posterior entryway will follow. It's something very simple to see. Who needs more big fastens at any rate?
- **No More Dial:** Eeek, what!? The first that comes to mind would be like, "What!? I utilize that dial constantly. I disagree; I change things mid-cut, and I adore that; I can, without issues, basically trade the fabric setting for the fabric dial. I adore my fabric dial." Well, no stresses, my friends! The dial isn't required. The interruption catch is considered there. At the point when you ignore you are not cutting cardstock anyway and that are cutting vinyl instead, simply hit respite. Every one of the features is in the application and basically prepared to help you at whatever point you need them. I do love this new design.
- **The Cartridge Space Has Been Dispensed with:** They took out this opening to make the instrument stockpiling greater. In any case, no stress. On the off chance that you have cartridges you have not matched up to Plan Space, and you aren't at present close to home and your Explore to fix your cartridges, you can get an outside cartridge drive to allow you to adjust your cartridges. On the off chance that you have just adjusted your cartridges with your present-day Explore machine, at that point, you're good to go; you don't have to rehash the technique with this new machine. Your structures are, as of now, convenient in Configuration Space. Remember, when you purchase a cartridge through Structure Space, you individualize these plans as indistinguishable, as though you offered the good cartridge. So, you don't need the cartridge space at any rate.

The Cricut Maker is a ravishing new expansion to the Cricut group of cutting machines. Regardless of whether you are looking to make sewing projects, paper assignments, or something totally unique, the Cricut can enable you to cut it! You'll be making artworks for every single event with your Cricut.

Chapter 2: Explaining the Different Models of Cricut Machines

It is safe to say that you are addressing the thought of obtaining a new Cricut but have yet to decide on which one to get. Perhaps you're, in any event, pondering one of the more established designs from a family member or friend; however, you end up awake all night without having a clue about what the machine does. All things considered, you are in the perfect spot; I couldn't imagine anything better than to educate you concerning the different Cricut machines that are currently available.

At the very beginning, there were only 2 models available from the earliest starting point. The Cricut machines are all produced and manufactured by Provo Craft. We also saw the first models working solely with a cartridge, although there were many other advances in innovation available. This didn't force Provo to be behind the game, though, because they were able to turn out some machines that are phenomenal today. They will be listed by models that are no longer available first and then the newer models. The reason for this is that several crafters out there continue to use models that are now outdated and have no need for the use of a computer in order to be able to create their projects.

Individual (Unique) Cricut Electronic Shaper Machine

- Cost: 99$–199$ (never again sold).
- Mat measurements: 6x12 inches.
- The cut the size of the genuine picture has measurements of 11 ½ inches wide and 5 ½ inches high.
- The Figuring gadget no longer needs a PC for it to function. The utilization of cartridges is all it needs as they are inserted into place with the end goal for pictures to be cut. It would be ideal if you note that Cricut cartridges are presently being changed for computerized pics just, and soon, they may be suspended totally.
- A button with four functions controls the cutting blade on the Cricut.
- It works perfectly with other Cricut models.
- It works perfectly with Art Room by Cricut.

The Cricut Maker

- No longer available for purchase.
- Mat measurements: 6x12 inches.
- The picture size cut is 5 ½ inches high by 11 ½ inches wide.
- This Cricut does not require a computer. Cartridges are used and are inserted into space with the goal of photographs to be removed. It would be good if you notice that Cricut cartridges are presently being changed for advanced photos, so they soon could become obsolete.
- An 8-position selector is attached to help with the movement of the blades.
- It has a few similarities to the Vagabond.
- It works perfectly with Art Room by Cricut.
- Tall picture function.
- Mode for website fitting.
- It cuts and focuses photo.
- The "Flip" picture works.

Expression 1

- Cost: 199$–399$ (never again sold).
- Mat measurements: 12x24 inches and 12x12 inches.
- The picture size is 23 ½ inches wide by 11 ½ inches high.
- No computer is needed. Cartridges are utilized and are part of the space with the goal for pictures to be cut. Please note that Cricut cartridges are presently being replaced with a more advanced technology, so they may be totally discontinued.
- It includes an 8-position selector for the movement of the blades.
- The machine is all around coordinated with Cricut Tramp.
- It works perfectly with Art Room by Cricut.
- Tall picture function.

I might want to call attention here that the Cricut Expression 1 additionally works with outsider programming. This is then again not acknowledged by Provo Craft, and so it voids the warranty of your machine. If this is exactly what you are looking for and you plan to use it for that purpose, then I truly propose to recommend that you proceed to get one of the more up-to-date models of the Cricut machines.

Expression 2

- Cost: 149$ (never again sold).
- Please note that the Cricut cartridges are currently being supplanted by computerized photos just so they would potentially be totally discontinued.
- The machine is appropriate with Cricut Wanderer.

Cricut Maker Machine

- Cost: $399.
- They are available in sizes of 12x24 inches or 12x12 inches.
- The Max Genuine Picture measurements are at least 11 ½ inches high and 23 ½ inches wide.

- It allows a low number of pictures to be printed.
- It includes a Versatile Instrument Framework for cutting a great many more materials. It is not quite the same as past machines and uses another Rotatory Blade for fabric and a Fine-Point Blade for thicker materials.
- It includes many advanced sewing designs.
- It can be configured and programmed remotely.

Chapter 3:
Explaining How to Use a Cricut Machine

Have you purchased another machine and were currently befuddled through Cricut's setups? Cricut machine setups can be somewhat astounding. From Cricut Maker setups to Cricut Explore Air 2 setups, we are responding to most of the inquiries you may have about where to get started with your machine.

Cricut Beginning Aid

So you got a Cricut, and you're presumably eager to begin, but you aren't sure where to start. Perhaps all you do is gaze at the holder (because, let's get genuine, the compartment has possibly been staying there for some time). I'm here to let you know that you are not the only one! Your Cricut machine is going to improve your work and life! What's more, even in spite of the fact that it can be difficult at first, this data will help you get initiated with your Cricut cutting machine in 5 simple steps!

Step 1: Open the Box of Your Cricut!

This one may, moreover, seem somewhat strange, yet on the off chance that you are like me, once in a while, that is the hardest part! Or potentially, you opened the container and set it on a table, and it's simply been staying there. Simply get out the Cricut machine, set it up, and plug it in. I fathom you can do it!

Step 2: Use Cricut Design Space

You'll be expedited to use Cricut Design Space once you download Cricut Design Space. Cricut Design Space is the free programming project that accompanies every single Cricut workstation and is cloud-based. In case that you have a record of your configurations, you can log in from any PC or device that has the Cricut Design Space programming program or application. You'll have the option to get to most of your projects any place on any device you are signed in.

There are three sorts of Cricut records: Free records and paid records. For the time being, you sign in with a free record and hold on, sign in with the Cricut Access paid membership plan. There are masses of components in Cricut Design Space that are allowed to utilize when you begin. As you begin to utilize it increasingly, at that point, you can decide whether you need to pursue membership.

Likewise, be sure to agree to the "New Machine Arrangement" assistant in Cricut Design Space to get your Cricut configuration.

Step 3: Discover Amateur Cricut Classes

Attempt to discover beginner guidelines from friends who also have Cricut machines. You can show up for guidelines at art stores, like Michaels or JoAnns, or a local scrapbook shop. If you don't have a specialty shop close by, you can still look for help on the Web.

My favorite web page to find classes online is SkillShare. I've researched instructional exercises on everything from cell phone Photography to Photoshop and Learner Watercolor classes. At the present time, they have a free preliminary for 2 months, and you can take the same number of guidelines as you need. It's an appropriate place to begin for free!

Step 4: Become More Acquainted with the Cricut Design Space Language

Once in a while, the scariest thing about the utilization of the Cricut is picking up information about the language. Since every one of your tasks is made utilizing the Cricut Design Space program, you will have more inclinations to redo your undertakings. Yet, that limits picking up information of the Cricut language and what each component can accomplish for you. "Weld," "Connect," "Cut," "Gathering,2 what does all that mean?

Step 5: Make Your First Cricut Project

First, it's an ideal opportunity to make something! You can make the principal essential test by following the instructional exercise in Cricut Design Space. This will also help you gain proficiency with the fundamentals of the Cricut Design Space. Make a point to watch the "New Machine Configuration" data, and it will invite you to do your first project.
Then, make it a stride likewise and begin out on some exceptional beginner projects. You can investigate my Cricut Task Pinterest board to get additional thoughts. I have uploaded my favorite amateur activities for the Cricut. Pick one of those and make one today! You have to set up to conquer your Cricut workstation for all your crafting projects.

Learn Advanced Cricut Skills

On the off chance that you are hoping to take your Cricut journey to the next level or are looking to make a touch of doing side business, I grasp a way that can enable you to arrive. The Cut Above SVG Configuration Course is extraordinary. Jennifer Maker shows you how to make your very own cut records that are the establishment for doing errands on a Cricut cutting machine. Before the end of the course, you will know about how to make 3D structures without any preparation. This is exclusively open a few cases a year (as a rule in the spring and fall), so jump on the shortlist to get informed when it opens.

Begin with Your Cricut

With these 5 stages, you can begin utilizing your Cricut to make amazing creations. Right now is an ideal opportunity to make time in your life to be imaginative while using your Cricut for your projects!

Pick, Adjust, or Plan a Project

When you log in to Cricut Design Space, you can click on Make It Now. You should think and plan before starting another project. Select one of your current projects, or create another one.

When your project is ready, click on "Make It" to start up the machine your machine. Load your cutting mat. Place your fabric on the cutting mat. Follow the rules in Configuration Space for stacking your cutting mat. Be sure to press the glimmering "Load" button after you place the mat on the machine so it stacks appropriately.

Press the "Go" button and let the PC get down to business!

When you press "Go" in Configuration Space, the Cricut connection on your PC will begin. Press it so the machine starts cutting.

The Cricut will get down to business. Configuration Space will tell you on the off chance that you need to change pens, cutting blades, or the cutting mat.

Appreciate Your Works!

At the point when the machine has finished cutting, writing, and scoring, you will be told by Configuration Space and glimmering lights on the workstation to remove the cutting mat. Press the button you used to stack the mat to now remove it. Take your finished work off the mat, and then you're ready to delight in it.

The Reason for Font Styles for Cricut Machines

Typically, Cricut offers its own special arrangement of font styles that can be utilized with Cricut machines. Yet, on the off chance that you experience that you have font styles that are never again adequate to convey copious varieties in your work, then you can purchase more Cricut font styles. There are 100s of exquisite font styles accessible. In any case, in the event that you do not utilize Cricut font styles anyway, the font styles mounted on your PC can be enough.

What Is Required to Use Font Styles in Cricut Machines?

To utilize any font styles in your Cricut Machine, you will need to install Cricut Design Space onto your PC. When this software is installed, it will precisely match up helpful font styles in your PC and make them accessible to be utilized in your Cricut machine.

How to Install Cricut Design Space™?

The installation procedure is practically identical to the installation of programs like a net program, a media player, and so on. Be that as it may, if this is the first time that you are installing a program on your PC, then follow the below steps to install Cricut Design Space™ on your PC:

1. Go to the folder where you have the Cricut Design Space™ installer.
2. Double click the installer file. The Cricut Design Space installation wizard will show up.
3. Click on the "Next" button to proceed.
4. Read the Acknowledge the Terms and Conditions file and then click on the "Next" button.
5. Click on the "Next" button to continue the installation procedure.
6. Again, click on the "Next" button.
7. Click on the "Next" button.
8. Click on the "Install" button to proceed to install Cricut Design Space™.

This is how to install Cricut Design Space™ on your PC. After it is installed, you can utilize any font style in your Cricut machine.

How to Use Font Styles in Cricut Machines?

After you have set up Cricut Design Space on your PC, you never need again to utilize something different so as to utilize the font styles on your PC. Simply start Cricut Design Space, and in the font styles tab, you will see all the font styles that you have previously adjusted. Select any of these font styles, and similarly, you can use the Cricut font styles. Note: In the event that you have downloaded some other font style family from the Web and want to use it in your Cricut machine, you have to research if you can use that font style in your machine.
This is the way to utilize any font style with your Cricut machine. We trust that this part has been valuable to you, and you will have the option to use any font style with your Cricut machine without any difficulty.

Cricut Machine Setup

All in all, where do you start from? Get your Cricut workstation out of the box now! I made a video about unpacking your machine and setting it up. Cricut has made it helpful for you. Presently, it is just dependent upon you to do it and start getting imaginative with your machine.

Cricut Design Space Setup

Below I have all you should know about setting up your Cricut machine:

1. Spot the webpage on the Cricut box.
2. Go to the webpage shown to start the setup.

This will walk you through setting up a Cricut account and downloading Cricut Design Space to your PC or cell phone.
The instructions will keep on walking you through your first project. Everything that you need to make your first project is incorporated with each Cricut machine. This makes the Cricut set up top-notch and easy to do! It also makes it easy to become familiar with your new machine.

How Would I Transfer My Own Pictures to My Cricut Machine?

Being in a situation to transfer your own photographs offers you loads of opportunities to make anything you need with your Cricut. You can include anything from straightforward, level jpeg pix to convoluted multi-layer vector records, and Cricut Design Space will naturally interpret them so you can print, cut, emblazon, or use them to support your Cricut projects!

Transferring Basic Images

1. To transfer any image to Cricut Design Space, first open Cricut Design Space in your internet browser.
2. Click on the "New" button in the upper left-hand corner to create a blank project.
3. At the bottom of the toolbar on the left is the "Upload" symbol. Click on that symbol to open the "Upload" tab.

4. From right here, you can include both a basic image (a single-layer image; for example, ".jpg," ".gif," ".bmp," or ".png") or a vector image (a multi-layer picture; for example, ".svg" or ".dxf").

Most images you see on the web are basic images, meaning that they are flat, single-layer images. They can have multiple colors and even appear to be 3D, but the actual image itself is made with pixels of different colors to give the appearance of shading or depth. These single-layer images can be created in programs like "Adobe Photoshop," "PicMonkey," "Canva," and other simple photo editing programs. Photos from your phone or camera are also basic, flat images.

Photographs from your phone or camera are also basic, level pictures. You can transfer ".jpg," ".gif," ".bmp," and ".png" files to Cricut Design Space, and they will all be transferred as single-layer images. Here's how to transfer a basic picture. From the "Upload" tab in Cricut Design Space, click the green and white "Browse" button. Then either drag and drop an image file into the window or click the green and white "Browse" button to open an image file. Once you choose a basic image to upload, it will show a preview on the left side and ask you to select the image type. You can choose from:

- **Simple:** This is for a super basic image with high-contrast colors and either a transparent or single-color background.
- **Moderately Complex:** This is for images with some details and multiple colors, but with good contrast between the subject of the image and the background.
- **Complex:** This is for detailed images with blended colors or shading/gradient (a little harder to work with because of the level of detail).

For this example, I chose "Simple" because it's a very "simple" design. Then click the green "Continue" button.

The next step is to "process" the image to make sure that only the parts you actually want to cut out make it into your project. You have three basic tools you can use to process the image:

- **Select and Erase:** This is like the magic wand tool in PhotoShop; it allows you to select an area or specific color in your uploaded image and erase it. If you click on the "Advanced Options" button, you can change the tolerance.
- **Erase:** This is just a standard eraser tool. You can change the size of your eraser using the slider on the left.
- **Crop:** You can crop away entire areas of your image using the crop tool.

I use "Select and Erase" for about 90% of the images I upload to Cricut Design Space; it's really powerful and really smart!

The next step is to decide what type of image you have, and give it a name. You can save your uploaded image as a "Print then Cut" image, or just as "Cut" image. If your original image has details in it (like a photo of your kids that you want to print first, or something where the colors are important, then cut), save it as a Print Then Cut image. If it is just a shape that you want to cut out, you can save it as a Cut image.

Give your image a name and add tags if you want, then click on the green "Save" button. Your uploaded image will appear in the "Recently Uploaded Images" section at the bottom of the "Upload tab." Just select your uploaded image and click on the green "Insert Images" button to add it to your project!

Transferring Vector Images

Vector images are image files with multiple layers, usually created in a program like Adobe Illustrator.

You can upload ".svg" and ".dxf" files to Cricut Design Space, and they will all be uploaded as multiple layers, with each image layer or color being separated into separate layers in Design Space.

Here's how to upload a vector image:

1. From the "Upload" tab in Cricut Design Space, click on the green and white "Upload Image" button.
2. Then either drag and drop an image file into the window or click the green and white "Browse" button to open an image file.
3. (Because vector image files contain all the image details within the file itself, Cricut Design Space can actually process these images for you automatically without you needing to do anything! You will see a preview of your image on the left, and after it's uploaded, each layer of color will be its own layer.)

    Just give your image a name and add tags if you wish, then click on the green "Save" button.
4. Select your uploaded image from the "Recently Uploaded Images" section, then click on the green "Insert Images" button to add it to your project!

You'll notice that when you insert a basic image, it will appear in black, but the vector image will appear in whatever colors were used in the original vector file. The basic image will be one single layer in the "Layers" toolbar on the right, but the vector image will be split into layers or colors.

In Cricut Design Space, different colors act as "layers," so when you go to cut this design, it will automatically split red, white, blue, and black into four different "cuts" so that you can cut them out of different colors or materials if you wish. If the SVG file you upload is all one color, Cricut Design Space will instead automatically split each layer into a separate layer/group in your project.

Vector images are a lot more powerful if you are planning to cut multiple colors or materials because the layers automatically translate into layers in Cricut Design Space. But for simple "Cut" or "Print then Cut" projects, uploading a basic image will work just fine!

Chapter 4: Explaining What Cricut Design Space Is and How to Use It to Create Your Own Custom Projects

Are you trying to learn everything about Cricut Design Space, and you don't even know where to start?

Learning a new hobby or skill can be intimidating at first. I get it; sometimes, we don't even know where to start because there's so much information out there, and it's just overwhelming.

For me, the best way to learn and master Cricut Design Space is from the beginning!

You see, when you have a clear concept of what every icon and panel is for, then you can truly dig in and start exploring further and further.

Sometimes we are quick to jump from project to project—Hey! That's ok too! BTDT.

However, I think that knowing your work area will help you take your creativity to a whole new level.

The purpose of this chapter is to teach you and show you an overview of every icon and panel of the Cricut Design Space Canvas Area.

Before we dig in, let's learn what the Cricut Design Space Canvas Area is: The Cricut Design Space Canvas Area is where all of the magic happens before you cut your projects.

Design Space is where you touch up and organize your creations. In this space, not only you can use and upload your fonts and images, but you can also use Cricut's premium images and fonts via individual purchases, Cricut Access, and Cartridges.

Now that we got these concepts out of the way, let's get started!

Cricut Design Space Canvas Tutorial for Beginners—What's Everything for?

Investing in a Cricut is futile if you don't learn how to master Design Space because you will always need this software to cut any project.

In my opinion, Cricut Design Space is an excellent tool for beginners, and if you have no experience with any other design program, like Photoshop or Illustrator, you will find that although it looks overwhelming, it's quite easy. You guys, if I can do it, you can too!

On the other hand, if you have some previous experience with any of the Adobe Creative Cloud apps or Inkscape. You will see that this program is just a breeze. Design Space is mainly to touch up your projects and create minimal designs with shapes and fonts.

If you want something more sophisticated, you are going to need your own designs or Cricut Access. That's a membership where you get access to their supergiant library.

When you log into your Cricut Design Space account and want to start or edit a new project, you will do everything from a window called "Canvas."

The canvas area in Cricut Design Space is where you do all the editing before you cut your projects.

I get it! There are so many buttons, options, and things to do that you might feel lost. Don't worry; I am here along the way, cheering you up and encouraging you to keep going.

In this chapter, you are about to learn what "every single icon" on the Canvas area is for. To keep everything in order and easy to understand, we are going to divide the canvas into four areas and four colors:

- Yellow Top Panel—Editing Area
- Blue Left Panel—Insert Area
- Purple Right Panel—Layers Panel
- Green Canvas Area

Tip: This is not a short chapter, so I encourage you to get a cup of coffee with some donuts or cookies, if possible.

Top Panel Cricut Design Space

The top panel in the Design Space Canvas area is for editing and arranging elements on the canvas area. From this panel, you can choose what type of font you'd like to use; you can change sizes, align designs, and more!
This panel is divided into two sub-panels. The first one allows you to save, name, and finally cut your projects. And the second one will enable you to control and edit things on the canvas area.

Sub-Panel #1—Name Your Project and Cut It

This sub-panel allows you to navigate from the canvas to your profile and projects, and it also sends your completed projects to cut.

Toggle Menu

When you click on this button, another whole menu will slide open. This menu is a handy one. However, it's not part of the canvas, and that's why I won't be going into a lot of detail.
Basically, from here, you can go to your profile and change your photo.
There are other useful and technical things you can do from this menu, like calibrating your machine and blades and also updating the firmware/software of your device.
You can also manage your subscriptions from Cricut Access, your account details, and more.
Note: On the "Settings" option, you can change the visibility and measurements of the canvas; this is explained better at the end of this chapter when I explain all about the canvas area.

Project Name

All projects start with an "Untitled" title. You can only name a project from the canvas area after you've placed at least one element (image, shape, etc.).

My Projects

When you click on "My Projects," you will be redirected to the library of things you have already created; this is great because sometimes you might want to recut a previously created project. So, there's no need for you to recreate the same project over and over.

Save

This option will be activated after you've placed one element on your canvas area. I recommend you save your project as you go. Although the software is on the cloud, if your browser crashes, there goes your hard work with it!

Machine

Depending on the type of machine you have, you will need to select either the Cricut Joy, Maker, or the Cricut Explore Machine; this is very important because on the Cricut Maker, you will find options that are only available for that particular machine.
So, if you have a Maker and you are designing with the Explore option on, you won't see the tools that are for the Maker.
The different options are for "Operation." (I will be covering on this chapter.)

Make It

When you are done uploading your files and ready to cut, click on the "Make It" button. Down below, there's a screenshot of what you would see. Your projects are divided into mats according to the colors of your project.
From this window, you can also increase the number of projects to cut; this is great if you are planning on creating more than one cut.

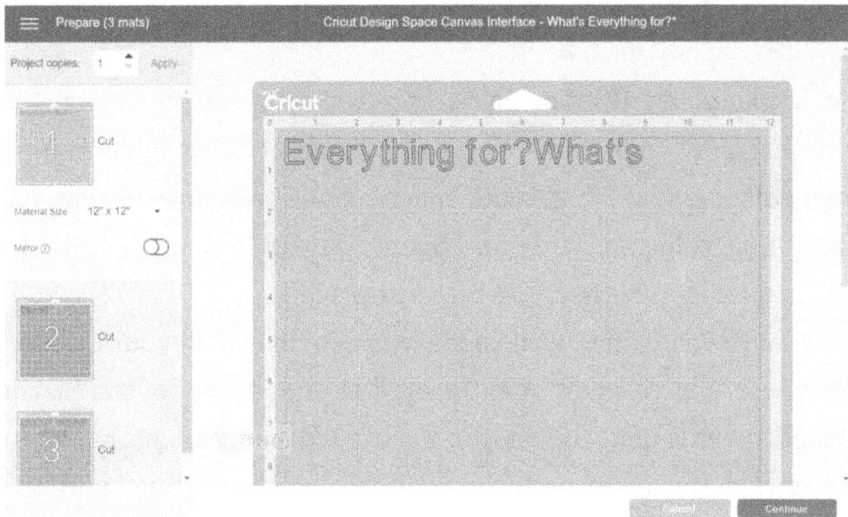 When "Make It" is clicked, this is what appears.

Subpanel #2—Editing Menu

It's extremely useful, and it will help you to edit, arrange, and organize fonts and images on the canvas area.

Undo and Redo

Sometimes, while we work, we make mistakes. These little buttons are a great way to correct them.
Click "Undo" when you create something you don't like or make a mistake. Click "Redo" when you accidentally delete something you didn't want to delete or modify. (If only there were something similar for life itself!)

Operation

This option will tell your machine what tools and blades you are going to use.
Remember that depending on the machine you have selected on the top of the window (Maker, Explore, or Joy), you will have different options.
Right now, there are nine operations: Basic Cut, Wavy, Perforate, Pen, Foil, Score, Deboss, Engranve, and Standard Print, then Cut.
If you have a Cricut Maker, all options will be available; if you have an Explore, you will be able to cut (Basic Cut), draw (Pen, Foil, and Score), and last, if you have a Cricut Joy, you will only be able to cut (Basic Cut) and draw (Pen).

Here is a more in-depth explanation of some of those functions:

- **Basic Cut:** Unless you uploaded a JPEG or PNG image to the canvas, "Basic Cut" is the default operation that all of your elements on your canvas will have. Therefore, this means that when you press "Make It," your machine will cut those designs.

  With the "Basic Cut" option selected, you can change the color of each layer to represent the materials you will use when you cut your projects.

- **Draw (Pen):** If you want to write on your designs, you can do it with your Cricut! When you assign this operation, you will be prompted to choose any of the Cricut pens you have (You need specific pens unless you have a 3rd-party adapter). When you select a particular design, the layers on the canvas area will be outlined with the color of the pen you picked.

  With this tool, when you click "Make It," your Cricut will write or draw instead of cutting.

  Note: This option "doesn't" color your designs.

- **Draw (Score):** Score is a more potent version of the scoring line located on the left panel. When you assign this attribute to a layer, all the designs will appear scored or dashed.

  This time, when you click "Make it." Your Cricut won't cut, but it will score your materials.

  For these types of projects, you will need the scoring stylus or the scoring wheel. However, keep in mind that the wheel only works with the Cricut Maker.

- **Standard (Print then Cut):** The "Standard Print Then Cut" option is mainly to be used for printing and patterns.

  Print is by far one of the best features that Cricut has because it allows you to print your designs and then cut them. This is fabulous, and honestly, it's what motivated me to get a Cricut in the first place.

  I design tons of printable for kiddos and adults, and for taking photos, I had to cut every single little thing!

  Ahhhgggg, I seriously wanted to cry every time. I am a lefty, and scissors really make my hands hurt. So, the Cricut is a live saver for me.

  Anyway, we are getting back to the printing option. When this operation is active, after you click "Make It," first, you'll send your files to your home printer and then have your Cricut do all the heavy cutting.

Another excellent option for this is "Patterns"! You guys, this is so cool. Use Cricut's choices, or upload your own. You can add a pattern to pretty much any kind of layer. The imagination is your limit!

Let's say it's Valentine's Day. You can make a beautiful card with an already created pattern from Cricut Access (membership, not free) or your own. Then print and cut at the same time. Thank you, Cricut!

Select All

When you need to move all of your elements inside the canvas area, you may struggle to select them one by one. Just click "Select All" to select all the elements from the canvas.

Edit

This icon will allow you to cut (remove from the canvas), copy (copy the same item, leave original intact), and paste (insert copied or cut elements on the canvas area) items from the canvas. The Edit Icon has a drop-down menu. The cut and copy option will be activated when you use have a selection of one or more elements from the canvas area. The Paste option will be enabled once you copy or cut something.

Offset

Offset, in Cricut Design Space, is a tool that allows you to create a proportional outline inside and outside of text, images, and shapes. The offset tool is quite handy when you need to make projects like stickers, cake toppers, or any other design in which you may want to add a "stand-out" effect.

Align

This function allows you to align all your designs, and it's activated when selecting two or more elements.

- **Align Left:** When using this setting, all the elements will be aligned to the left. The furthest element to the left will dictate where all the other elements will move towards.

- **Center Horizontal:** This option will align your elements horizontally. This will entirely center text and images.
- **Align Right:** When using this setting, all of your elements will be aligned to the right. The furthest element to the right will dictate where all the other elements will move.
- **Align Top:** This option will align all of your selected designs to the top. The furthest element to the top will dictate where all the other elements will move.
- **Center Vertically:** This option will align your elements vertically. It's handy when you are working with columns, and you want them organized and aligned.
- **Align Bottom:** This option will align all of your selected designs to the bottom. The furthest element to the bottom will dictate where all the other elements will move.
- **Center:** This option is a very cool one. When you click "Center," you are centering, both vertically and horizontally, one design against another one. This is particularly useful when you want to center text with a shape like a square or a star.

Distribute

If you want the same spacing between elements, it's very time consuming to do it all on your own, and it's not 100% right. The "Distribute" button will help you out with that. For it to be activated, you must have at least three elements selected.

- **Distribute Horizontally:** This button will distribute the elements horizontally. The furthest left and right designs will determine the length of the distribution. This means that the items that are in the center will be distributed between the most distant left and right designs.
- **Distribute Vertically:** This button will distribute the elements vertically. The furthest top and bottom designs will determine the length of the distribution. This means that the items that are in the center will be distributed between the most distant top and bottom designs.

Arrange

When you work with multiple images, texts, and designs, the new creations you add to the canvas will always be in front of everything. However, some of the elements of your design need to be in the back or front. With the arrange option, you can organize the elements very easily.
Something great about this function is that the program will know what item is on the front or back and when you select it. Design space will activate the available options for that particular element. Cool right?
These are the options you get:

- **Send to Back:** This will move the selected element all the way to the back.
- **Move Backward:** This option will move selected the item just one step back. So if you have a three-element design, it will be like the cheese in a cheese sandwich.
- **Move Forward:** This option will move the element just one step forward. Typically, you would use this option when you have four or more items you need to organize.
- **Sent to Front:** This option will move the selected element all the way to the front.

Flip

If you need to reflect any of your designs in Cricut Design Space, this is a great way to do it.
There are 2 options:

- **Flip Horizontal:** This will reflect your image or design horizontally. Sort of like a mirror; it's handy when you are trying to create left and right designs. For example, you are building some wings and already have the left side. Then, with "Flip," you can copy and paste the left-wing, and voilà! Now you have both (left and right) wings!
- **Flip Vertical:** This will flip your designs vertically. Kind of like you would see your reflection on the water. If you want to create a shadow effect, this option would be great for you.

Size

Everything you create or type in Cricut Design Space has a size. You can modify the size from the element itself (when you click on it). However, if you need an item to have an exact measurement, this option will allow you to do so.
Something essential is the little lock. When you increase or reduce the size of an image, the proportions are always locked. By clicking on the small lock, you are telling the program that you don't want to keep the same dimensions.

Rotate

Just like size, rotating an element is something you can do very quickly from the canvas area. However, some designs need to be turned on a specific angle. If that's the case for you, I recommend you to use this function. Otherwise, you will spend so much time fighting to get an element angled the way you want it to be.

Position

This box shows you where your items are on the canvas area when you click on a specific design.
You can move your elements around by specifying where you want them to be located on the canvas area. It's handy, but it's a more advanced tool.
Personally, I don't use it that much because I can get around better with the alignment tools I mentioned above.

Font

When you click on this icon, you can select any font you want to use for your projects. You can filter them and search for them at the top of the window.
If you have Cricut Access, you can use any of all the fonts that have a little green "A" at the beginning of the font title.
However, if you don't have Cricut Access, make sure you use your system's fonts; otherwise, you will be charged when you send your project to cut.

Style

Once you pick your font, you have the option to change its form.
Some of the options you have:

- **Regular:** This is the default setting, and it won't change the appearance of your font.
- **Bold:** It will make the font thicker.
- **Italic:** It will tilt the font to the right.
- **Bold Italic:** It will make the font thicker and tilt to the right.

Font Size, Letter, and Line Space

I can't express enough how "amazing" these options are, especially the letter spacing.

- **Font Size:** You can change it manually from here. I usually just adjust the size of my fonts from the canvas area.
- **Letter Space:** Some fonts have a considerable gap between each letter. This option will allow you to reduce the space between letters very quickly. It's seriously a game-changer.
- **Line Space:** This option will tackle the space between lines in a paragraph. This is very useful because, sometimes, I am forced to create a single line of text because I am not happy with the spacing between lines.

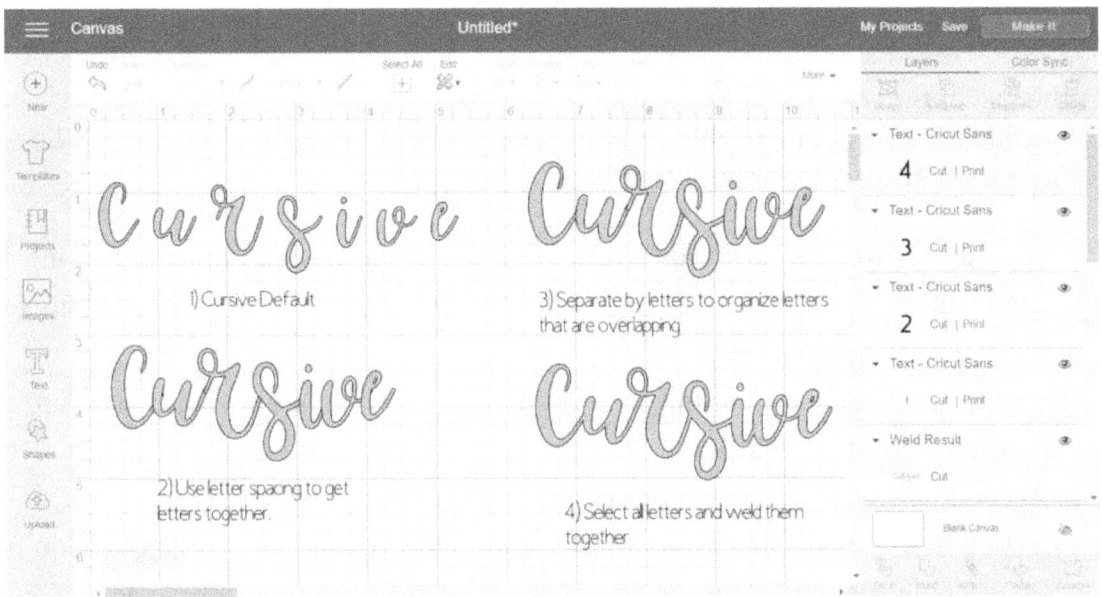

Font Size, Letter, and Line Space

Alignment

This "Alignment" differs from the other "Alignment" I explained above. This option is for paragraphs.
These are the options you have:

- **Left:** It aligns a paragraph to the left.
- **Center:** It aligns a paragraph to the center.
- **Right:** It aligns a paragraph to the right.

Curve

This option will allow you to get extra creative with your text!
With this function, you can curve your text. The best way to learn it's by playing with the little slider.
When you move the slider to the left, it will curve the text upwards, and when you move it to the right, it will bend the text inwards.
Note: If you move the slider entirely to the left or right, you will form a circle with your fonts.

Advance

Advance is the last option on the editing panel.
Don't be intimidated by the name of this drop-down menu. Once you learn what all the options are for, you will see they are not that hard to use.

- **Ungroup to Letters:** This option will allow you to separate each letter into a single layer (I will explain more about Layers down below). Use this if you have plans to modify every single character.
- **Ungroup to Lines:** This option is exceptional, and it will allow you to separate a paragraph into individual lines. Type your paragraph, then click on ungroup to lines and there you have it: A separate line that you can now modify.
- **Ungroup to Layers:** This one is the trickiest of all of these options. This option is only available for multi-layer fonts. These kinds of fonts are only available for individual purchases and/or Cricut Access.

A multi-layer font is a type of font that has more than one layer. These fonts are great if you want to have some shadow or color around them.

What if you like a font that is multi-layer, and you don't want the added layer? Just select your text and then click "Ungroup to Layers" to separate every single layer.

Left Panel—Insert Shapes, Images, and More

With the top panel (that I just explained in detail), you are going to edit all of your designs. But where do they all come from? They all come from the Cricut Design Space Left Panel.

This panel is all about inserting shapes, images, ready-to-make projects, and more. From here, you are going to add all the things you are going to cut.

This panel has seven options:

- **New:** This is used to create and replace a new project in the canvas area.
- **Templates:** This allows you to have a guide on the types of things you are going to cut. Let's say you want to iron vinyl on a onesie. When you select the template, you can design and see how the design would look like.
- **Projects:** This is used to add ready-to-make projects from Cricut Access.
- **Images:** This is used to pick single images from Cricut Access and cartridges to create a project.
- **Text:** This is used to add text to your canvas area.
- **Shapes:** This is used to insert all kinds of shapes on the canvas.
- **Upload:** This is used to upload your images and cut files to the program.

There's something fundamental that you need to consider on this panel: Unless you have Cricut Access, Cricut images, ready-to-make projects, and Cricut fonts cost money. If you use them, you will have to pay before you cut your project.

Now that we saw a little preview of what everything is for on this panel, let's see what happens when you click on each of those buttons.

New

When you click on "New," and if you are already working on a project, you will receive a warning on top of the window asking you whether you want to replace your project or not.

If you want to replace your project, make sure to save all the changes from the current project; otherwise, you will lose all that hard work. After you save your project, a fresh new and empty canvas will open up for you to get started.

Templates

Templates help you visualize and see how your project will fit on a particular surface. I think this feature is just out of this world.
If you want to personalize fashion items, this tool is marvelous because you can select sizes and different types of clothing, plus they also have a lot of various categories that you can choose from.

Projects

If you wish to cut right away, then "Projects" is where you want to go! Once you select your project, you can customize it; or click on "Make It," and follow the cutting instructions.
Tip: Most of the projects are available for Cricut Access members, but you can purchase them as you go. However, there are a handful of projects "free" for you to cut, depending on the machine you have. Just scroll to the bottom of the categories' drop-down menu and select the machine you own.

Images

Images are perfect when you are putting together your own projects, and with them, you can add an extra touch and personality to your crafts.
You can search by keyword, highlighted categories, themes, people, places, and occasions.
Cartridges are a set of images that you need to purchase separately. Some of them come with Cricut Access, and some do not. (Brands such as Disney, Sesame Street, Hello Kitty, etc. are not part of Cricut Access).
Under "Highlighted Categories" Cricut has "free" images to cut every week.

Text

Anytime you want to type on the canvas area, you will need to click on "Text," and then a little window that says "Add text here" will open on the canvas.

Shapes

Being able to use shapes is essential! With them, you can create simple and less complicated yet beautiful projects.

There're nine shapes you can choose from:

- Square
- Triangle
- Pentagon
- Hexagon
- Star
- Octagon
- Heart

The last option is not a shape but an amazing and powerful tool called "Score Line." With this option, you can create folds and score your materials.
If you want to create boxes or love everything about card making, the Score Line will be your best friend!

Upload

Last, but not least! With this option, you can upload your files and images. The internet is filled with them, and there are tons of bloggers that create projects for free.

Right Panel—Learn All about Layers

To set you up for success, and before I explain to you what every icon is all about on the "Layers" panel, let me give you a little introduction of what a layer is.
Layers represent every single element or design that is on the canvas area.
Think of it like clothing; when you get dressed, you have multiple layers that make up your outfit, and depending on the day or time of year, your outfit can be simple or complex.
So, for a freezing day, your layers would be underwear, pants, shirt, jacket, socks, boots, gloves, etc., and for a day at the pool, you would only have one layer, a swimsuit!
The same happens with a design because, depending on the complexity of the project you are working on, you'll have different types of layers that'll make up your entire project.
For example, let's pretend that you are designing a Christmas Card. What would this card have?
Maybe a text that says Merry Christmas, a tree, the card itself, and perhaps an envelope as well?
My point is that all the little designs and elements that are part of that project are layers.

Some layers can be modified; however, other layers, like JPEG and PNG images, can't; this is because of the nature of the file or the layer itself.

For instance, a text layer can be converted into other types of layers; but when you do that, you'll lose the ability to edit that text.

As you go, you will learn more about what can or can't do with layers.

I hope that gave you a good idea of what a layer is! Now let's learn what every single icon is for on this right panel.

Group, Ungroup, Duplicate and Delete

These settings will make your life easy when moving things around the canvas area, so make sure to play around with them.

- **Group:** Click here to group layers. This setting is handy when you have different layers that make up a complex design.

  Let's say you are working on an elephant. Most likely (and if this is an SVG or cut file), the elephant will be comprised of different layers (the body, eyes, legs, trunk, etc.); If you want to incorporate extra shapes and text; most likely is that you will be moving your elephant across the canvas area a lot.

  Therefore, by grouping all the elephant layers, you can make sure that everything will stay organized and nothing will get out of place when you move them around then canvas.

- **Ungroup:** This option will ungroup any grouped layers you select on the canvas area or "Layers" panel. Use this option if you need to edit (size, type of font, etc.) a particular element or layer from the group.
- **Duplicate:** This option will duplicate any layers or designs you have selected on the "Layers" panel or canvas.
- **Delete:** This option will delete any elements you have selected on the canvas or "Layers" panel.

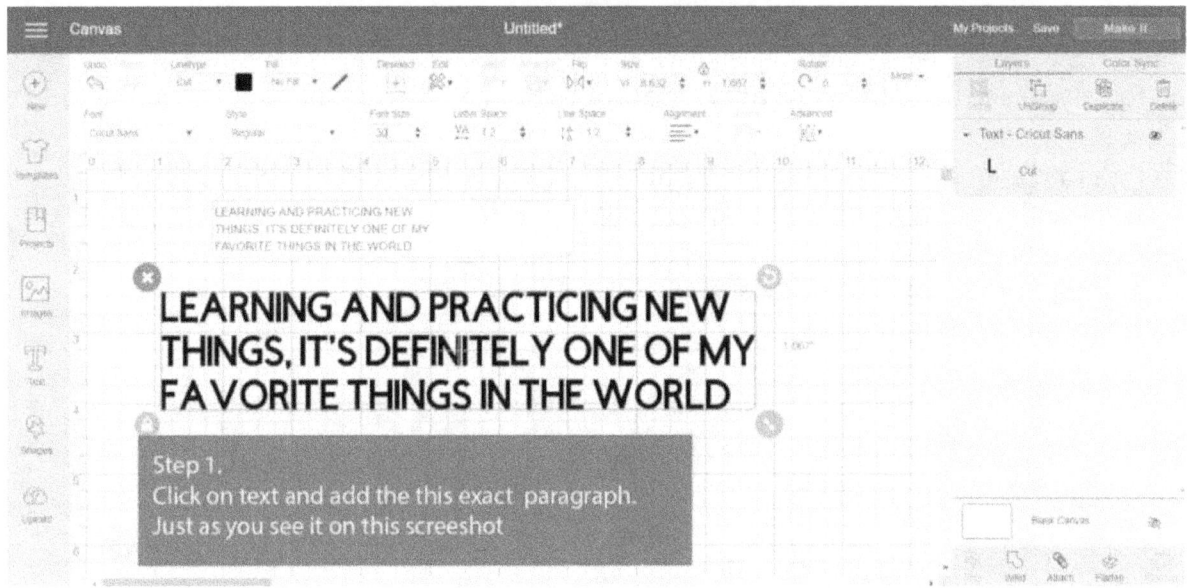

Group, Ungroup, Duplicate, and Delete

Operation

Every item on the "Layers" panel will show what operation you are using (Basic Cut, Wavy, Perforate, Pen, Foil, Score, Deboss, Engrave, and Standard Print, then Cut).

Layer Visibility

The little eye that appears on every layer on the "Layers" panel represents the visibility of a design. When you are not sure whether an element looks good, instead of deleting it, click on the little eye to hide that design.
Note: When you hide an item, the eye will have a cross mark.
Tip: By clicking on a layer and dragging it, you can move a particular design on top or under. You could say that this works like the "Arrange" option (sent to the front, back, etc.).

Blank Canvas

This "layer" allows you to change the color of your canvas if you are trying to see how a particular design looks with a different color.
This setting's power is unleashed when you use it along with the "Templates" tool because you can modify the color and the options of the template itself.

Slice, Weld, Attach, Flatten, and Contour

These tools you see here are incredibly important! So make sure you master them to perfection.
I won't go into a lot of detail on them because they deserve chapters on their own. However, I will give you a brief explanation of what they are all about by using the graphic down below.

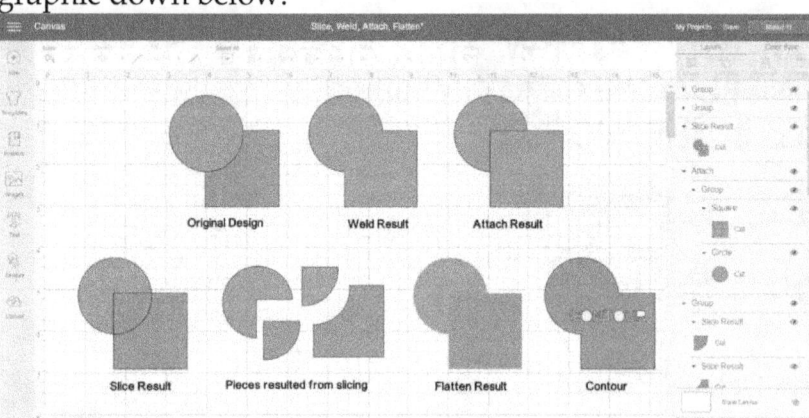

Slice, Weld, Attach, Flatten, and Contour Info-Graphic

As you can see in the graphic, the original design is a pink circle and a teal square. Now let's see what happens when I use all of these options.

- **Slice:** The slice tool is perfect for cutting out shapes, text, and other elements from different designs.
  When I selected both shapes and clicked on slice so you can see that the original file got all cut up. I did so to show you what the final outcome was. I copied and pasted the "Slice Result" and then separated all of the pieces that resulted from slicing.
- **Weld:** The welding tool allows you to combine two or more shapes in one.
  I selected both shapes and clicked on Weld so you can see that I created a whole new shape. The color is determined by the layer that is on the back, and that's why the new shape is pink in color.
- **Attach:** Attach works like grouping layers, but it's more powerful.
  I selected both shapes and clicked on attach so you can see that the layers just changed color (determined by the layer that is on the back). However, the shapes are connected, and this attachment will remain in place, even after I send my project to be cut.
- **Flatten:** This tool is extra support for the Standard Print Then Cut setting.

You see, when you have "Print then Cut" activated, that change applies to just one layer at a time. But what if you wish to do it to multiple shapes at the time?

When you are done with your design, select the layers you want to print together as a whole and then click on "Flatten."

When you are done with your design (you can't reverse this after exiting your project), select the layers you want to print together as a whole and then click on "Flatten."

In this case, the element became a Print Then Cut design, and that's why it isn't showing a black edge (where the blade will go through) anymore.

- **Contour:** The Contour tool allows you to hide unwanted pieces of a design, and it will only be activated when a shape or design has elements that can be left out.

For this example, I combined the original design in one shape with the weld tool, then I typed in the word "contour" and sliced it against the new shape, and then I used the "Contour" tool to hide the inner circles of the two letters "O" and the inner part of the letter "R."

Color Sync

Color Sync is the last option of the "Layers" panel.
Every color on your canvas area represents a different material color. If your design has multiple shades of yellows or blues, are you sure you need them?
If you only need one shade of yellow, just click and drag the tone you want to get rid of and drop it on the one you want to keep.

Canvas Area

The canvas area is where you see all of your designs and elements. It's very intuitive and effortless to use!

Canvas Grid and Measurements

The canvas area is divided by a grid; this is great because every little square you see on the Grid helps you to visualize the cutting mat. In the end, this will help you to maximize your space.

You can change the measurements from inches to centimeters and turn the grid on and off when you click on the top panel toggle and then select "Settings." (You can see this toggle menu right at the beginning of this chapter).
A window will pop up with all the options.

Selection

Anytime you select one or more layers, the selection is blue, and you can modify it from all four corners.
The "red x" is for deleting the layers. The right upper corner will allow you to rotate the image (although if you need a specific angle, I recommend you to use the rotation tool on the editing menu).
The lower right button of the selection, "the small lock," keeps the size proportional when you increase or decrease the size of your layer. By clicking on it, you are now able to have different proportions.

Zoom in and out

Last but not least, if you want to see on a bigger or smaller scale (without modifying the real size of your designs), you can do it by pressing the "+" and "-" signs on the lower-left corner of the canvas.

Conclusion

Now that you successfully made it through "Cricut for Beginners," you will be a whole lot more confident in knowing what your Cricut machine is, how to work it to make projects, and know what material types you can use for your crafting ideas.
You will also be able to share the ideas you learned here with family and friends, as well as be able to create many items for others, all with your Cricut machine.
With that said, let's hope that you received a lot of information that is useful and will continue to give you and your friends years of fun with the many crafts that you make.

www.ingramcontent.com/pod-product-compliance
Lightning Source LLC
Chambersburg PA
CBHW081422080526
44589CB00016B/2641